Quotes to Inspire & Empower Women and Girls

Quotes to Inspire & Empower Women and Girls

CREATING A MINDSET *for* SUCCESS

Purpose Driven

Passion Powered

Prosperity Bound

By Patricia B. Freeman

Greensboro, North Carolina

Quotes to Inspire & Empower Women and Girls...Creating a Mindset for Success

Published by Pat B. Freeman, LLC

PO Box 4781, Greensboro, NC 27404

pat@patbfreeman.com

Email: pat@patbfreeman.com

Website: patbfreeman.com

LinkedIn: www.linkedin.com/in/patbfreeman

Facebook: www.facebook.com/PatBFreemanLLC

Twitter: @patbfreeman

ISBN-13: 978-0578181158
ISBN-10: 0578181150

First Edition by Pat B. Freeman, LLC printing, May 2016

Dedication

This publication is dedicated to my sons, Sterling and Styles, and all women and young girls who dare to dream. Dream big and be empowered because we are all created to live with purpose, passion, and prosperity. And when we support and believe in one another, we can do things that have never been done. I hope the words in this book will be an inspiration to all who read it.

To my Mom and sister (Neat), who have passed but are alive in my heart.

This is also for you.

Table of Contents

Quotes to Inspire & Empower Women and Girls

It Takes A Village: Affirmations From Men

Resources

Introduction

Throughout my journey of experiences and life's lessons as a mother, educator, and entrepreneur – and in observing other women, I've learned that "life
happens" to all of us. But even when it happens, we must continue to persevere. Through our will, determination, and inherent power, we will achieve any goal we set out to accomplish. The decision is ours.

This book of quotes is written to inspire you to walk every day in your greatness. You are built in the image of excellence. Therefore, no matter what comes your way, do it with purpose and passion. Then prosperity, in all forms, will open up to receive you. Be prepared to embrace what is already in you.

We must continue to lift up young girls, mothers, daughters, sisters and others with principles and values that create a mindset for success. Every person who contributed to this book, both women and men, are walking in their greatness
and live by the statements that they share in their quotes. Although you cannot see their faces, their hearts are revealed through their words.

The guiding principles behind my desire to write this book stem from the definitions of the words purpose, passion, and prosperity. They are not mere words. They are words with meaning that can result in a lifestyle of success and fulfillment. *It's time to become:*

Purpose Driven
The feeling of being determined to do or achieve something

Passion Powered
A strong feeling of enthusiasm or excitement for something or about doing something

Prosperity Bound
The condition of being successful or thriving; especially economic well-being

~Webster Dictionary

WOMAN POWER

Quotes for Women by Women

I AM

Passion Powered.
Abundantly blessed.
Spiritually led.
Secure in my skin.
Inspired to greatness.
Open to Opportunity.
Never to quit.

~Pat B. Freeman

The strength of a woman is not measured in muscles, but in her ability to accomplish the unthinkable.

Lena Murrill Chapman
Educator, Professional Coach

Quotes by Pat B. Freeman

Author, Speaker, Educator, Entrepreneur

"Let other people do what they like. But I choose to do what I love."

"When obstacles seem to block your way, or a door closes, find another door. Remember, if there is a will, there is a way. That means there is Always a way. You just haven't found it yet."

"When you have crystal clear clarity on the WHAT and the WHY, it clears the way for the HOW."

"To empower a woman, is to empower a nation."

"Where there is Passion, there is Possibility and Purpose."

"Know who you are...Know whose you are...Know your purpose...
Take Action!"

"Success depends on you. The power of decision resides in you. You get to choose..."

"Reach for the STARS. To discover your purpose and live your dreams, you must seek His will and follow your passion."

"Are you busy?
Or are you being productive? Which are you..."

"Let His work in and through you be the testimony of His goodness."

"Don't expect a harvest if you never planted any seeds…
INVEST IN YOU."

"Show respect
before you expect respect."

"Why not DREAM BIG.
Take action.
That's how you make dreams come true."

"I now know exactly what I can do.
I can do anything I put my mind to.
The universe will do the rest."

"You're only as free as the box you put yourself into.
So don't put yourself in a box."

"Recognize that you can't do it all.
But **you can** do your best."

"You'll get your breakthrough
When you know you're not through
Until something breaks."

"You don't have to see it to believe it.
But you must Believe it to Achieve it."

"Your ticket to success is you!"

"Don't chase a dream...
Build it!"

"Take action on your dreams...
It's the only way to fly!"

"Be overcome by FEAR…
Or find Freedom through FAITH."

"When the going gets tough, that's your cue to hold on…
Success awaits!"

"Know who you are
And whose you are…
That's the power of identity."

~

"It has been done. It can be done. And I can do it!"

~Mazie Butler Ferguson
Attorney, Candidate for US Congress 13th District

"You may be only 1 small match but you can start an explosion. Believe in the power you have to change the world."

~Kristie Notto
Author, Podcast Host, AwesomeSauce Marketing

"You can't wish for what you want; you have to **work** for what you want!"

~Elizabeth Colen, CPLC
Entrepreneur

"All blessings come from God. Look to Him for your strength and delivery."

~Thelma Boyd
Banking, Retired

"A successful woman is one who knows what she wants and works hard to get it."

~Dr. Randy Whitfield
President of Adult Education Training

"Do what you love. And success and money shall follow."

~Clara Carter
Author/Business Owner

"Successful retirement takes Godly wisdom and purposeful planning!"

~Violet Cross
Retired Educator/Wife/Mother

"Despite what you might think or how you might feel about yourself, you are a masterpiece made by God."

~Leah-Shaleis Cross
Wife and Mother

"A wise person seeks WISDOM."

~Violet Cross
Retired Educator/Wife/Mother

"When you accept man's definition of who you are, he puts you in a box. When you accept God's definition of who you are, He empowers you so that no box man makes can contain what you do for Him."

~Cynthia Lewis
Retired Educator

"Being empowered isn't outside of us, but inside of us."

~Sandra Leverette
Retired Educator

"Never let shortcomings or misfortunes make you lose sight of your goals. Obstacles should intensify your objectives so that you may master the art of the comeback."

~Mary Ann Bradley
Social Services Case Worker

"Continue to be a beacon of light."

~Dr. Brittney Clinton
Educational Practitioner

"You can't quit and keep going at the same time."

~Violet Cross
Retired Educator/Wife/Mother

"If you stop growing you may miss the possibility that changes everything."

~alorrinda Michieka
Project Manager

"Your secrets are your road to success. Your mourning is your road to independence. Tell it. Release it. And cry no more."

~Dorothy Louise
Hope & Empowerment Speaker for Children

"Sparkle Where You Are

ONE small act has the potential to change the world.
ONE idea can spark a movement.
ONE person can make a difference."

~Jennifer H. Gray
Motivational Consultant, The Sparkle Project

Life can be a real challenge.

But despite the struggles, twists, and turns,

There is joy, hope, and possibility on the other side.

So don't give up. Don't ever quit.

~Pat B. Freeman

"Being intelligent is gaining knowledge. Being smart is applying and using the knowledge.

Because we are human beings, and though God has perfectly made us, we are not perfect. We make mistakes.

Gain knowledge and learn from your mistakes. What you do with that knowledge determines how **smart** you are. If you keep making the same mistakes and do not change anything, nothing changes...you do not grow. Learn something every day, and apply your knowledge to your life lifting up the One Who lifts up you so you can lift up others."

~Cynthia Lewis
Retired Educator

~

Quotes by Ashlee Moena Boyd
Human Resources

"Be willing to surrender what you are, for what you could become."

"Excellence is the result of caring more than others think is wise, risking more than others think is safe, dreaming more than others think is practical, and expecting more than others think is possible."

"We are God's masterpiece (work of art, workmanship). Our salvation is something only God can do. It is his powerful, creative work in us. If God considers us his masterpieces, we dare not treat ourselves or others with disrespect or as inferior work."

Embrace your faults and flaws
because, without a bump or a starch,
without a love and a loss;
you would not have a beautiful story, with chapters of
strength, guidance and understanding.

You would not be who you are.
With the light that surrounds you.

Embrace your faults and flaws
because without them, you would not be a magnificent work
of God!

~Ashlee Moena Boyd

When a woman is empowered,
The world changes from the inside out.

Lena Murrill Chapman
Educator, Professional Coach

Quotes by Paula Hopwood
Inspirational Speaker/Coach/Author

"Sometimes you have to truly let it go in order to find it."

"Sometimes things are not as you see them. Dig deeper for
your truth."

"Take that chance
Take that opportunity
Spread Your Wings
And Soar."

"Embrace it till you make it."

"In order to remember
Who we truly are
We need to let go of
Who we think we are."

"I broke up with my past
Embraced my future
And now I live my dream."

"If your path is no longer paved
Remember
It's still a path.
Journey on."

"The best thing I ever did was I started to believe.
And the first thing I started to believe in was me."

"First seek wisdom
Then allow it to happen."

"Sometimes you just have to take that chance.
Then work that chance
So it works for you."

~Paula Hopwood

~

Quotes by Dr. Gloria J. Savage-Early
Author, Educator, Singer, Runner

"Treat people with respect, kindness and love.
You never know what they are going through."

"The compassion we have for others is an opportunity for
God to propel us forward toward our destiny in life."

"I see my dreams and they are only dreams;
faith makes my dreams realities when I trust God."

"I have a VOICE.
It is my instrument of praise.
I must be careful to use it wisely."

"My mother, Beatrice Walton Savage, taught me to focus on what I have and what I can do, not what I don't have and what I can't do.
When I follow those instructions.
I see the hand of God in my life."

"Trying times are opportunities for us to show God how much we really trust Him."

"A smile is a gift that God uses to lift the hearts of those that see your beautiful smile."

"Love is a powerful action that heals, restores, and takes people to places where life is full of joy and peace."

"Please" and "thank you" are often influential words that tell the hearts of people that you are a thoughtful person.
They are not influential words when the person who speaks them doesn't have the right motive."

"In helping others, I am helping myself to become a helper in a world that needs help."

"Forgiving is a choice that heals both the giver and the receiver of the forgiveness."

"Remember: Treat people with respect, kindness and love. You never know what they are going through."

~Dr. Gloria J. Savage-Early

~

IT TAKES A VILLAGE

AFFIRMATIONS FROM MEN

MAN POWER

Quotes of Empowerment by Men

"In our time…

In our space…

And with the grace of God,

We can make a difference."

~Mr. Joe L. Dudley, Sr.
Founder of Dudley Products, Inc.

"Never let your self-worth be determined by the coins that rattle in your pocket."

~Emilio Antonio Guevara
President & CEO, SB Fuller & Joe L. Dudley Sr. Foundation

"When you decide on what you truly want in life, go on a faith fast. That's where you starve your fears, doubts, and critics out of your life and replace them with faith in God, yourself, and your dream."

~Dr. Joe White
Business Consultant and Speaker

"Everyone in the room is not on the team. And everyone on the team is not in the room."

~John Steward
Engineer/Entrepreneur

"There's nothing more powerful than a woman who believes in her dreams. Become that woman today!"

~Joe Dudley Jr.
Entrepreneurial Business Coach

"Only God has the Devine power of creation. But it is the female who births love, devotion, strength, and tenderness. Like a precious diamond, she has the capacity to light up the world as bright as the sun, moon and stars. She is queen and mother of the universe..."

~William Geter
Father/Former College Administrator

"Live with Purpose because there is Greatness within you. Your Success is your Choice."

~Marlon Smith
Educational Consultant

"If you don't feel completely ready to try an idea you have in your head, do it anyway."

~LaGuardia Cross Jr.
Husband/Father/Artist

"Be the best version of yourself and you'll inspire others to do the same."

~Larrnell Cross
Host/Producer/Poet

"I have raised my daughters to know that they are the life-force of humanity and that they are the most powerful beings on the planet. They know they can allow a man to join them upon their journey to aid with the missions; however, they also know they're more than equipped to travel alone to achieve their vision!"

~Robert Lancaster
Entrepreneur

"Faith and fear cannot operate at the same time. Choose Faith."

~Marlon Smith
Educational Consultant

"Where there is change, there is opportunity. Since change is constant, there is always opportunity."

~Jimmy J. Davies
Entrepreneur

"If an elephant is asleep in the jungle, anything can happen to that elephant. But when the elephant is awake and moving forward, nothing in the jungle can stop it or slow it down. What we fail to recognize is the elephant in us."

~Dwight D. Brown
Motivational Speaker

"Empower yourself with the knowledge of your strength and talents, as producers and nurturers of the human race…based on the many roles you carry out in a day. Be great unto yourself."

~Dr. Michael E. Harris
College Administrator

ME

I can be **M**ore
I can be **E**nough
I can be me…

~Johnson Bradley, Jr.
Administrative Officer II

"Jesus has the answer to all life's questions and concerns."

~LaGuardia Cross Sr.
Rev., Retired Educator, Husband/Father

"Every good and perfect gift comes from God. And He created man in His own image. And woman was taken from the center of man. This brings me to the conclusion that a woman is the center of the universe. All things were birthed through her. Man born of a woman will have but a few days, and they will be filled with trouble.....but, the good news is......trouble won't last always."

~Rev. Theodore Stevens, Jr.
Minister/Funding and Consulting

"The words of a women, communicated in the right way, will make a man do awesome things. He will walk through a wall and not even know it's there. The most powerful thing a woman has is her words. The sound of her voice can be like jet fuel to a man."

~Dwight D. Brown
Motivational Speaker

From My Sons

Sterling B. Freeman, College Student/Rap Artist

"Knowledge is only potential power.
It doesn't become power until it is organized into a plan of
action."

"Information cost. But it pays for itself."

"Good things come to those who wait.
But success only comes to those who try and persist."

"Criticism is a negative statement with no solution."

"When you first see a diamond, it's in its purest form. When it comes from the ground, everything is right with it because it's exactly how the world intended it to be now. When Man gets it and burns it, cuts it, molds it, and shapes it into the jewelry that we wear, the diamond is technically damaged. But, in turn, it's more beautiful than before. It's the same thing with people. We never come out the same innocent person we started off as. But God allows us to go through hell, or a process that molds, cuts, and shapes us so we come out more beautiful on the other end. So, in some way, we were beautifully damaged."

~Sterling B. Freeman

~

Styles B. Freeman, College Student

"True confidence is not found in the reassurance of one's strengths but in the ability to assure positivity, despite one's weaknesses."

~

Be Who You Are...

~Dr. Linwood M. Carver
Ministry

"The power that is already in you will amaze you. But you must try in faith."

~Dr. Gregory T. Headen
Pastor

Resources: From the Author

Learn about my products and other information at patbfreeman.com

Confident Speaker Training

5-Week Coaching Program
Website: PatBFreeman.com

Online Course: 3 Steps to Becoming a Confident and Engaging Speaker.
Website: Udemy.com

Ebook: God Sets You Up Manifesto
Website: Amazon.com

Visit my website to schedule a Complimentary Breakthrough Session: PatBFreeman.com. Or email me for speaking engagements: pat@ patbfreeman.com

Look for my Upcoming Launches – Coming Soon!
- **New Book:** *Passion to Profits – The 4Ps to All-Star Entrepreneurship*

- **Online Academy:** *Passion to Profits Entrepreneurship Dream-Building Academy™*

About the Author

Patricia B. Freeman, *Building Passion-Powered Lives*℠

Pat B. Freeman is a John Maxwell certified speaker, trainer, and coach with more than 20 years as a college administrator where she managed over 125 faculty and staff and served up to 3500 students annually. She is an author, serial entrepreneur, educator, and the founder of Pat B. Freeman, LLC – a training and coaching business. Pat (aka The Dream Builder) is passionate about empowering women and others to move from "stuck to clarity" in areas of leadership, career, and personal growth. Her goal is to inspire you to have a successful and fulfilled life by doing what you love and stepping out to achieve your Big Dreams.

Pat delivers passionate, impactful, and enthusiastic coaching and training events that empower women, executives, and the workforce towards success. She is innovative and enjoys working with projects that create amazing solutions. With her energy and enthusiasm, she energizes people, inspires action, and promotes success for you and your organization.

As a personal and executive coach, Pat provides breakthrough results for her clients as an experienced mentor. They learn to lead with passion, purpose, and profits.

She is eager to share her expertise with you in the following areas:

- Inspirational & Keynote Speaking
- Passion Leadership Development
- Workforce Development & Training

Pat holds a Masters' degree in Educational Administration from Campbell University and Bachelors' degree in Theatre from Florida State

University. Other certifications: Certified Program Planner (CPP, LERN), HUB, and Lean/Six Sigma Yellow Belt. Pat is also the National Association of Professional Women (NAPW) Greensboro Chapter President.

Pat resides in North Carolina, is a native Floridian, and is the mother of two young adult sons, Sterling and Styles.

PAT'S PRESENTATIONS ARE IDEAL FOR...
Professional Women, Entrepreneurs, Corporate Executives, Professional Organizations, Colleges, Universities, High Schools, and Young Adult Groups

Acknowledgements

To each person who submitted a quote, it is because of you that I was able to meet my challenge to compile and publish this book within 7-14 days. You helped me turn what should have been impossible into possible.

To my family, I thank you for always believing in me. Thank you to each woman who submitted a quote, and to the men (in support of this effort) who readily sent your quotes of empowerment. Your expressions of wisdom and passion will become the spark that ignites the flame in women and young ladies everywhere. I am grateful to all of you. Together we are now "published to empower." We became the village.

To Eugene Freeman, the father of my children, I thank you for your support when technology worked against me, and I had nowhere to turn to fix the problem, you took care of it.

A special thank you to Marlon Smith, Kristie Notto, Dr. Gloria J. Savage-Early, and Tony Freeman for rescuing me with your support and nudge. Thanks for your generosity and expertise. You responded when I needed you most. Without you, this book would still be a dream or a wish.

Special Recognition

Mr. Joe L. Dudley Sr., Founder of Dudley Products Inc., thank you for your willingness to share one of your many mantras of success. When I asked, you said yes without hesitation or question. Your name and life serve as a legacy, model, and testament of inspiration and empowerment to all who encounter you.

Permissions

Lena Murrill Chapman
Mazie Butler Ferguson, Attorney
Kristie Notto
Elizabeth Colen
Thelma Boyd
Dr. Randy Whitfield
Clara Carter
Violet Cross
Lea-Shaleis Cross
Cynthia Lewis
Sandra Leverette
Mary Ann Bradley
Dr. Brittney Clinton
alorrinda Michieka
Dorothy Louise
Jennifer H. Gray
Ashlee Moena Boyd
Paula Hopwood
Dr. Gloria J. Savage-Early

Mr. Joe L. Dudley, Sr.
Emilio Antonio Guevara
Dr. Joe White
John Steward
Joe Dudley Jr.
William Geter
Marlon Smith
LaGuardia Cross Jr.
Larrnell Cross
Robert Lancaster
Jimmy J. Davies
Dwight D. Brown
Dr. Michael E. Harris
Johnson Bradley, Jr.
LaGuardia Cross Sr.
Rev. Theodore Stevens, Jr.
Sterling B. Freeman
Styles B. Freeman
Dr. Linwood Carver
Dr. Gregory T. Headen

.